WWJD

AND OTHER POEMS   SAVANNAH SIPPLE

SIBLING RIVALRY PRESS
DISTURB/ENRAPTURE
LITTLE ROCK, ARKANSAS

WWJD and Other Poems
Copyright © 2019 by Savannah Sipple

Cover image: Lorenzo Cafaro

Author photograph: Rebecca Dayle Ashby

Cover and interior design: Seth Pennington

Sibling Rivalry Press, LLC
PO Box 26147
Little Rock, AR 72221
info@siblingrivalrypress.com
www.siblingrivalrypress.com

ISBN: 978-1-943977-59-8

Library of Congress Number: 2018960659

First Sibling Rivalry Press Edition, March 2019

This title is housed in the Rare Book and Special Collections Vault of the Library of Congress.

for you, my love

WWJD

AND OTHER POEMS   SAVANNAH SIPPLE

TABLE OF CONTENTS

I

15   I Wanted You to Fuck Me,

16   Cant

17   Darling, you're a stain

18   Finished

19   When Those Who Have the Power Start to Lose It, They Panic

21   What We Tell Ourselves

28   All I Know of Coal

II

30   Box[h]er

31   After Seeing a Topo Map of my Childhood Stomping Grounds Hanging in a Colleague's Home

33   Baby, You're a Blight

34   Pork Belly

35   Evangelism BINGO

36   Pass/Back

39   Catfisting

40   Love Letter to the Boys in the First Class I Ever Taught

41   I text my friend one night, say *I want to do something stupid*

43   Thirst

44   A List of Times I Thought I Was Gay

47   An Open Response Question About My Parents' Marriage

48   Wannabe

49   Rain, Love

50   Somewhere There's Her Tongue

III

52   [Jesus and I have lunch]

53   WWJD / about fear

54   WWJD / on prayer

55   [Jesus is my best girl friend, my dutch boy]

56   And the Word Was God

57   WWJD / at the bar

58   [Jesus and I are on a break]

59   Jesus and I Went to the Walmart

61   WWJD / about letting go

62   Jesus Signs Me Up For a Dating App

63   WWJD / about my fat body

64   Jesus Shouts, *Amen!*

65   WWJD / about love

66   [Jesus rides shotgun]

"Two or three things I know for sure, and one is that I'd rather go naked than wear the coat the world has made for me."

Dorothy Allison, *Two or Three Things I Know for Sure*

I

I Wanted You To Fuck Me,

baby, I picked you for the bed   of your pickup, wanted you
in the woods, Natty Light and cigarette breath—wanted you
to say *god,*   *I love your tits*. It came down to camouflage.
I rode your four-wheeler fast—I wanted it,   love,   and you
could have given it to me   at the bonfire with leaves in my hair,
in the locker room after the game—you could have named your place,
honey, and I'd a been there with bells on. I'd have screamed your name
eyes shut wide open like I meant it, begging you   *please*   bang me straight.

Cant

My left eye is stronger than my right, so I tilt
the gun to that side. This is called canting.
Bub's been to war and come home   to teach me
to take care of myself. He has knowledge
I don't, says a .45 is different than my .22, but not
to be afraid of it or the one he hip packs.
The 1911 weighs my hand down, makes me
hold tight. I'm afraid   of backfire, of a black eye,
of blood.   The paper target tied to the tree
has holes in all the right places. *Damn, you ain't half
bad, sis.*   Men call girls *sis* here, women, too,
even when they want to fuck them. I never wanted
to learn, grew up afraid of the guns in the house,
but I like the way each bullet slides into place
when loading, each bullet blasts into the paper
vandal.   I am sick and thrilled at once,
like my fear got scared off but took me with it,
like Bub might choose to go back, like two wrongs
really can make   anything right.

Darling, you're a stain,

tobacco brown, round splashes on my hands,
my arms. The smell of Skoal—wintergreen—
lingers on my neck when you kiss on me, every crevice
an open spit cup, every dark flake a hickey.
Your fat plug tucked between teeth and lip.
My mouth a pouch where you spread white patches,
sores; I'm losing my voice. I've tried to wear you
close as overalls, arms locked heavy over shoulders.

I want to quit you cold-turkey,
but you stalk in spitting distance
and these yellowed stains on my fingers,
your fire-cured taint on my teeth,
I can't strip them,
can't scour your hills away.

Finished

You spent a night   legs up   in the back of a black truck
you remember the outline   sliver   of a boy's white back

he sat   legs dangling off the tailgate   smoking   you waited
for him to finish   sprawled out   while he finished   you did not

smoke   you did not drink   you drank enough
to get you in that cold metal bed   warmed up   your back bruised

your breasts sore   your throat raw   your roommate
sees your ragged hair   your saddlebag eyes   your stretched out

shirt   shakes her head   says *girl   you look like you been
rode hard   you look like you been hung up wet*

When Those Who Have the Power Start to Lose It, They Panic

They rut young girls. They come   to play.   They carry
their wallets   in front pockets,   checkbooks
in glove boxes.   Money.   No money.   They drink
beer.   They drink bourbon.

[She shouldn't have been drinking.]

They say shit like
boys will be boys   and   *you have to consider his side*
of the story   they mean his side of the story   is the only one
that matters   *there's two sides*   Girls should live
legs open and   mouths shut.   Go to church and dress up.

[What was she wearing?]

They four-wheel on weekends.   They ride in golf carts,
in Ubers,   on bicycles.   They get elected President.
They want their girls tough enough to ride shotgun, limber
enough to stretch   across backseats,   across laps,
against doors, in back alleys,   behind dumpsters.

[She was out too late.]

They want girls
sober enough to see,   drunk enough to see double,   *two sides!*
to moan,   *no* sounds like *yes* to their ears.   No
sounds like *yes* to their ears.   *Don't tell me no.*

[She had a mouth on her.]

                                        unless
we're talking about how twenty minutes might ruin the rest of
their lives, then *No!*—
wait—we don't deserve this.   *There are two sides!*
Listen to me!   They don't fuck up, do they?   They get up,
pay 120 thousand dollars,   walk away.

[She shouldn't have even been there.]

What We Tell Ourselves

I.

I show him my pay stub my weekly deposit
slip reasons for needing ten dollars this is
how it has to be This
    is working nine hour days
on my feet barely a break to come home
cook sweep mop wash wait
on him This
    is watching it fall around me
him sitting while shingles fly with every wind
gutters hanging loose leaking the back porch
needing the new gate This is him
       watching me
while I push mow rake leaves rake limbs this is him
this is his and I have no business asking
for help or money I shouldn't expect him to

the woman's place is to submit this
is fitting to the Lord

II.

[You can walk away
   and not look back]

III.

I'm too tired It's too expensive It was
his time to go I'll pray for you I had no
idea this was coming I've never raised
my voice or a hand to her She
has another feller The water is safe
Things are different
for a girl You can't do that I won't
let you I will knock your head off
I will take your car keys Do you
hear me I don't want to I'm not able to
She's wanted this for a long time She
asked for it
                              deep down
I come by it natural I come by it honest

IV.

[You can stay
          and survive]

V.

You'll never get married if you can't handle a man
wailin' on you   if you don't change
your attitude   don't shut up   don't
wear more dresses make up   if you don't learn to cook
don't stop being bossy   you better stop trying to show
how smart you are   stop tearing your legs up
playing sports, men like legs   stop sleeping
in sports bras, men like big breasts like your mother's
things are different for a girl   whatever this is
                              you'd better get over it

VI.

[You can leave]

VII.

I never wanted to stay I never wanted to
leave I never wanted to come back to gravel dust
I could not wait to leave I could not breathe
in the shadows I could not stand
the good country boys could not stand
the bible-thumping teenage girl humping
men I never could keep a secret
their shit-eating grins scratch-my-back politics
I know I will never meet people
as honeysuckle good as home
I know city neighbors won't never love me
as much I know what the good country
people say I know the good curvy road
I know how my skin tightens
when I have to go home I don't want to
go home I don't know where
home is I don't know if I love
the mountains I don't know if I hate
the mountains I love to drown
in the mountains I hate the crooked
mountains I love the mountains I hate
the mountains I love the mountains I hate
the mountains I love

VIII.

[It's a choice]

IX.

On the long dry days I wish I had hit you
I wish I had reared back as you screamed
I'll knock your damned teeth out
I wish I had let it fly I wish I'd
cocked my fist to your jaw right
as you claimed
I'll do it   *I will*

On those days I wake with the copper taste
of hate in my mouth When I can't
sweat it out cold I can't hold it
under the creek of me
I know I don't know
which I hate more
your lack of follow-
through or my own

X.

[Our anger is a lantern This little light
of mine]

XI.

Hang it in the family room

Man puts his hand to the flinty rock
*   and overturns mountains by the roots.*
He cuts out the channels in the rocks,
*   and his eye sees every precious thing.*
He dams up the streams so that they do
*   not trickle,*
*   and the thing that is hidden he brings*
*   out to light.*

But where shall wisdom be found?

XII.

[It's our fault]

XIII.

Rid her of topsoil   cleanse the skin
blast it open with knife   with dynamite
[The things we mine out are what kill us]
Needlewire your way to the seam   dragline tissue
swift   strive for clean margins   Place small clips
metal clips to mark your spoil   Don't over burden
her with waste   use a drain for the slurry
What would we save if we didn't destroy   the breast
Follow up with sponge baths support groups
radiation bumper stickers Then you can
reclaim what is yours

XIV.

[You can come back]

XV.

She always was a little bit quare they'll say
when you show up at the funeral home
with a full-on lezzie pompadour
black dress and tights be damned
Still you'll smile and tell them you're doing
just fine   even after the good church folks
stare at you side-eyed and whisper *backslider*

XVI.

[You can forgive]

XVII.

When it all goes to hell, the holiest
among them turn on you first   will
open a red-spined hymnal   sing
It is well [it is well] with my soul [with my soul]
It is well it is well with my soul

XVIII.

[It's not our fault]

XIX.

Once the mountains loved us. Once we loved the mountains.

All I Know of Coal

This is what happens when you cut the world in two: it turns
on you. We all die: cancer, copper water, no money,
meth, oxy, percocets, loss: a job or love, too much or too little
Jesus, mountain blasting zones—where we blow
ourselves apart.

Box[h]er

I was nine
Father claimed he'd knock my   goddamn head off
I jacked a boy's jaws   for calling me fat in gym class

In fifth grade
a girl smacked me first [I'm not a fighter—I swear]
I stood sycamore solid for years
while Father threatened
while girls on the ball team tried to   knock me down
They couldn't   I ran my mouth
to get them   anyone
to hit me   please   give me a reason
I was kind until I wasn't   Once
I started to slip that was it

The same chick goaded me   for years
until a literal push   a shove   in my back
                    [I could have been a lover]
My fist loved the side of her head
that kiss   smack of her hand   across my jaw   that
magnetic pull   until a teacher pulled us apart
eyes blazing like animals: We wanted each other
We yearned to hurt each other   so much   we ached

Later I helped separate two girls
They clung to each other's hair   Long hair
flew out in clumps   They jerked so tight
my head hurt   When one threatened to whip me   too
the basketball team set her straight

Solid ground those bitches

After Seeing a Topo Map of my Childhood Stomping Grounds
Hanging in a Colleague's Home

"Cartographers solve the problem of representing the three-
dimensional land surface on a flat piece of paper by using contour
lines, thus horizontal distances and vertical elevations can both be
measured from a topographic map."
—Idaho Museum of Natural History, Digital Atlas

Once, when I was a kid, to scare a bear, my father walked one
side of the trail and fired a rifle. The bear ran down the other side.
The mouth of the trail came out at the edge of the woods in front
of the house—that low dip-line was the home-run fence I aimed
for when we played baseball in the yard. The bases were trees and
home plate was right in front of our playroom windows. If you
rounded third, you always made it home cause we'd get our asses
beat over broken glass.

That was our benchmark, the one thing we knew:
he could beat us.

I knew the difference between a rabbit burrow
and a snake hole, but I was scared
of both—spent hours
perched around the shaded incline
between yard and woods,
knew both contained something
that could kill me.

Once I flipped a go-cart turning out of our drive too sharply.
Once I drove a four-wheeler straight into a tree. I once pitched
head over handlebars off my bike onto the gravel road trying to
outrace a loose dog. A vertical exaggeration: the neighbor who

found me thought I'd been hit by a car. Mom sat me in the garden tub, poured two bottles of rubbing alcohol all over my wounds to stop the threat of infection.

At basketball practice, I once refused to take a charge and the guard, shorter than me, stood nose to chestbone, said *do you know who you're messing with?* At home, bruises littered my ribs. At home, an agonic line split my arm after every time my father stood in my face and screamed *Do you know who you're talking to?* One inch equals ten miles.

I was fifteen and had a higher ACT score
than the point guard,
a senior. A line.
I was top in my class.
A line.

All lines.

Once I hit a line drive into my brother's chest. Twice his fist found my nose. A relief: every time we hurt each other, we cried. The contours tighten: I wrecked my truck, flipped a golf cart, crashed my car, kept telling myself I was lucky. When I was little, I kept bronchitis. My father gave me vodka for the cough. My lungs on fire. My kidneys on fire. My house on fire, years later, felt like a line, elevated, one that would bleed me dry, scar me, one that would leave me

marked.

Baby, You're a Blight

Your silks, those thin, sweet strings
stick to me, get caught in my hair. Days later, I find them
clutched to the canning stove, stuck to my bare legs, bare back,
the back porch where we fucked, unhusked
our skins where no one would see, tried to keep
from trailing them through the house. You take what you want
from me, say you're full as a tick burrowed in a hound.
Your grease coats everything you touch,
smudge-black on my skin, my clothes, the door.
Later you round on me, scream *I'll beat your ass.* You grab
and don't let go, leave your prints even when you're clean.
You're sorry. Again. I let you
peck me like a crow plucks corn, newly planted, fertilized,
straight from the ground. You work hard, want reward—
you till me in early morning, forget to use your finger
to see if I'm warm. Your ear rot molds me in place.
I can't leave by my own front door.

Pork Belly

Imagine you clutch the carving knife,
slice it under & against your own ribs—
one cut for every time they call you fat.
Take that meat, preserve it with salt
to season your beans—pinto, green.

In your hands, a bucket. The fat
sloshes, hot grease you collect
in coffee cans, glass jars, your dreams
dripping off your meat. This
is poverty: you save every drop.
Tell me, how many people

you trying to feed?

EVANGELISM

B	I	N	G	O
The Gospel	submit	bear	power	children
the Ministry	burdens	grace	tempts	sin
desire	cross	🙏	dress	comfort
fear	good news	set apart	closet	Jesus
born again	born gay	nature	proclaim	peace

Pass/Back

When I was four, my mother left me at the nursing home with my
grandmother & told her not to feed me, but I was hungry or I
complained I was, so Granny bought Cheetos. A damp orange
crumb glopped on my crisp white shirt. Before she could pick it
off, I swiped & spread it, and my mother lit in about how I didn't
need to eat anything, at all. *Look at her. Look at her*

shirt. I constantly check my back to make sure it's not *too* fat. My
back looks fat if my bra is too tight. A two-pack of extenders costs
eight dollars. If I size up, it'd mean a bigger cup, and I do well to
fill these C's. Even Lane Bryant has its limits. *A girl that fat
should have bigger tits.*

> Eight dollars can buy enough pinto beans to feed you all
> week. Wash pinto beans three times at least. Pick out
> the gravel. Soak them overnight.

The fat leaves my feet & calves first. It arrives home to my belly,
my thighs.

I notice back fat. Even thin women will have a small paunch when
they sit or slouch or bend. Fat spills out the back of bra straps on
really big women, or women who refuse to wear the bigger bra.

> Pressure-cook beans for ten minutes, throw in some
> fatback—the middlin meat—then finish cooking beans on
> the stove. The soup's the best part, soaked fat with pork
> flavor. Pass the cornbread.

My first diet came in the third grade. After we saw the doctor who
had two charts: one for height & one for weight. *If you make these
changes now, you might be able to lose the fat and never look back.*

Biscuits are carbs. Gravy is carbs. Pass the blackberry jam—carb.

If it seemed I'd gained weight, Mother'd stare & purse her lips. She'd pick my favorite foods off my plate, say *I just want a bite*. Like she could swallow my fat away.

When my 17th birthday came, the end of a liquid diet, I celebrated with a baked potato, no sour cream, no butter. She said, *Be careful so you don't gain back the fat.* The only thing worse than having to lose weight was it coming back.

I'd been eating cheeseburgers the whole four months, a mid-week treat. On the weeks I ate a cheeseburger, I lost five pounds—the weeks I didn't, I lost three. Pass the pickles.

Miracle Whip has a third of the calories and fat of mayonnaise. It was Miracle Whip only in our house & that stuff tastes like shit. I didn't know real mayo tasted different until I ate it on purpose in college. Pass the mustard.

Pass peanuts that might make my face breakout; pass whole milk, pass the milk fat; pass chocolate, also bad for my face; pass brie, hummus, avocado, Greek yogurt, the sour cream; pass potatoes mashed with butter, pass the fat fatty fat butter, pass it back around, the seconds, pass marbled steak, olive oil dressing, homemade croutons, pass fresh mozzarella, the pepperoni, thick crust.

My therapist says *where do you feel this trauma*. The tears answer, always, *in my back*.

Boxing makes me feel beautiful because muscles contract under my backfat ripples. I'm always the first to offer to carry a heavy load for someone else. I grip the steering wheel a certain way so my flexor muscles pop. Can you see muscle sinewed to muscle?

Backbones make the best taters. Pressure cook them together for 20 minutes and the meat will slide off the joints. That with those sweet greasy taters make a meal fit for a working.

I know what my back looks like from behind: pillowy.

I have weird food habits. I save my favorites for last and often by the time I get to them, I'm too full to enjoy them. I eat pizza with a knife and fork, cut my burgers in half, cut chicken meat from bones because it's gross to see a fat person enjoy her food. I carry Shout wipes in case anything drips. Food stains on clothes are a shame.

My favorite meal might be catfish and coleslaw, the salty fish with the slight hint of sweet in the slaw mixed with a kick of onion in a hushpuppy. Or lasagna, the way tomatoes and spices bed together atop cheese and meat. Or fresh green beans and cornbread. Or macaroni and tomatoes. Mustard greens and salmon patties. Taco salad. Toast and eggs. Baked buffalo chicken. Steak and sautéed mushrooms. I make a mean pot of chicken and dumplings and cornbread so good you don't even need butter. But a slice with molasses makes for a real good dessert.

I want to be marbled, so that if you were to slice me, you'd know what a good cut I am.

You see this fat body? Bite it. Let me fill you up.

Catfisting

I see you coming a mile away as I sit creek-cold
while you drink beer, catch fish with the boys.

I couldn't give a rat's ass about lures,
your rods, or how good you are

at reelin' them in. Your shit-eating grin doesn't work
on me. While you play with your scaling knife,

laugh at your own stories, loud, I'm already thinking
of her—by the time you look up to say *ain't that right* . . .

sweetie, I'm downstream, away from fingers
that hook me, angling for my own mudcat.

Love Letter to the Boys in the First Class I Ever Taught

I see you, sitting there in your letterman jacket, a Pepsi bottle
of tobacco juice wedged between your backpack and feet. I see it,
too, that chew tucked between front teeth and lip.
No, I don't want a nip. Yes, I know how to spit. I know you
parked in the woods all weekend, slept in the back of your truck.
I know you still had time for homework. Speed bumps:
your steel-toe boots in the aisles. You carry Axe body spray in your bag,
come to class sweating out both woodsmoke and semen. I have no desire
to see how big the barrel of your shotgun is. You sure as hell
aren't limber enough to have sex in a tree stand. I would not offer
extra credit, not even for a pity fuck. You talk of big bucks, of points,
of what you want to mount and whose skin you'd like to bury
yourself inside. If you've learned, it's on the power
of connotation, innuendo, your own. My silence did not save me.
Nor you. Come November, you beg me to pass you,
your daddy parking his souped-up F-250 double cab
outside the classroom to make sure you show up,
like your presence is the only thing that counts.

I text my friend one night, say *I want to do something stupid*

but what I do is order a double well drink at the bar
before the poetry reading, the one I almost left
cause 45 minutes after I order my drink
ain't nobody read a single damn poem, but I go
up to one of the guys who looks like he's from around here
but not from this bar and I say, *hey, are you Keegan?*
I wanna buy your book.
He's a cute guy with ice blue eyes and he hugs me.
Because I want to buy his book, this grit lit poet feller hugs me.
Twice. Kisses my cheek. Then he sells me a book & signs it.

I go home and eat Skinny popcorn, catch up
on *Grey's Anatomy*. What I do: coat my vibrator with coconut oil,
force it to loosen me, vibration on high. What I do: cry
cause I am afraid no one will ever love me. No one
has ever fucked me, not that it matters,
but on double well nights it does.

On double well nights I think about how I loved her
& wanted her, and I wonder if she loved me at all.
We slept curved into one another, her topless,
me in cotton pajamas. I wish I'd put my mouth
on her breasts that night on my couch,
when I ran kisses all over her back
or even when she flashed me at the ocean,
wave after wave of pink nipples. I wish I'd gone

topless in front of her, only I kinda did
but it was months later. My back was jacked up
and I didn't know why. No it wasn't cause I'm fat.
She kneaded tiger balm all over my back. It felt so good
it hurt. It hurt so much I teared up. She saw my back fat
& my side fat & probably even some belly fat.
All I wanted was to curl against her, my cheek to her skin.
Close. I want to be close. To anyone. I jump

41

when anyone touches me. When my friend hugs me
from behind as we cook together,
when Keegan pecks my cheek after his reading,
even when I touch my own fat self late at night,
in the dark, I cry & repeat to myself, *Yes, love. Yes, you are worthy.*

Thirst

I loved her from the first Sunday
she wore that green dress to church.
It was plain—cotton, forest green—
and hit a hair above the pale back
of her knees. The neckline came
low enough for me to see
something swelled underneath. I could see
my hands sliding up her legs, my hands
running up her sides, my hands slipping
that thing right off, quick, easy.
I loved that dress & her breasts
swelled underneath, the way
it clutched her body tight,
just enough to see her panty
line. My fingers wanted
under her panty line.
That dress was hot, but what
really got me was the way she wore
it, free, unconcerned, her body happy
with itself—the dress, only an afterthought.

A List of Times I Thought I Was Gay

1.

I gave a girl a handwritten copy of Peter Cetera
lyrics and it hurt me when she left them
in another girl's desk.

2.

I wrote a letter to my sports idol.
I wanted to be like her: a girl the boys
feared on the court.

3.

Whenever she made me wear a dress.

4.

I wore shorts & knee socks to the school dance
instead of a skirt. My friends laughed. A cute older boy
asked me to dance and his friends laughed.

5.

In the locker room, surrounded by sports bras
& ball shoes I felt no different. I looked.

6.

I cut myself with a straight razor.

7.

In the kitchen at church camp. I cleaned
dishes in three sinks: soap water, bleach, rinse.
Week after week, for years. I never felt clean.

8.

I wanted to hug someone.
I did not trust myself to hug someone.

9.

Boxing class. My body sore, my muscles
alive.

10.

When I saw you clothed.

11.

And imagined you naked.

12.

When I saw you naked.

13.

When I let myself hug you
in my mind and your arms
found my body, and we were
clothed & naked at once.

14.

I realized, if I wore makeup,
if I wore dresses,
she thought it meant I was straight.

15.

When the youth pastor decried our friend
might be dating a woman, my face flushed.

16.

When I wore my hair in a fauxhawk
then washed it out immediately.

17.

Every time I wanted to buy a new tie.

18.

When I notice your tight
shirt sculpted to your breasts,
your abs, your jutted-out hips.

19.

Every time a friend got married
and I went without a date.

20.

The first time I said
I'll never marry a man.

Then cried
when I realized I didn't have to.

An Open Response Question About My Parents' Marriage

In at least 500 words, prove or disprove the following statement: "I never hit her or went out on her. She had no reason to leave."

Wannabe

All your wet dreams begin the same way:
you pressed up on a boy, his hands
hold you right, slip beneath your skin, then

the shift: you're the boy with some girl
hemmed up against a door, her hips
grip-locked on yours. You know you should

be the girl tracing his contours of skin,
but then you've never done things the right way.
You make her moan, make her cling to you,

whisper commands. You bury your face
in the sharp corner where jaw
kisses neck. You wake and beg yourself

to forget the way she made you buckle.
You will learn, years later,
sin is another word for fear,

but even then you will be afraid
to let yourself love girls hungrily,
bold the way boys do.

Rain, Love

The rain loves the oak tree   you love her
slow, streams from top,   soft hair
soaks her wet drops   lavender
over each leaf,   the crook
runs damp   in her neck
hands down limbs   burrow there
kisses chest-bone trunk,   slumber
sinks in her,   kiss
quivers where drips slip,   lick
shivers as she slides   glide
way down to grass,   grasp
Do you see how   legs
she saturates you? Watch   wrap around her
droplet release drenched leaf—   taste her salt
drown in the trickle-taste.   finally breathe

Somewhere There's Her Tongue

In my mouth my love's tongue
is in my mouth my love
has her tongue somewhere else
in someone else's mouth she comes
home aroused, giggles, slips her tongue
in my mouth laughs *You're just like*
a guy her v-neck shirts
ride up to show lace panties
somewhere else my love's lace panties
are on the floor below my mouth
is her back where I kiss her spine
trace vertebrae with my tongue
somewhere in my arms she sleeps topless
beneath her nails my back my neck
she is underneath someone else somewhere
she says she doesn't want to share me
says she was somewhere coffee with a friend
my love lets me curve my body into hers
while she snores she sleeps somewhere
else somewhere different from where
she says my love turns her head
when I lean in to kiss her my love
says somewhere I am a lover
but lover I am not here.

[Jesus and I have lunch]

Jesus drinks PBR with his burger. I order bourbon and Ale-8, a BLT. As we leave, he says, *we should do this more often.*

WWJD / about fear

You feel her flame, small sparks
burn top down, her smoke
banks down, no fire line,
a line loss, no straight
stream cooling heat—
her back draft exposes your
fire load, your discharge flow.
It's too late, love. You're already
in her collapse zone.

WWJD / on prayer

Jesus would stop talking to my father / who last threatened
to hit me when I was six / no twelve / no twenty-six / who laughed

when he screamed and I started to cry / repeat / laughed when
I started to cry / who heard me say / repeat / he heard me

say / when he pinned me to the wall / or the couch / do not touch me /
he would touch me because I asked him not to / repeat / I asked him not to /

Jesus would say / *let go* / *throw yourself away* / *from that* / Jesus would take
one look / He'd say / *cut those ties* / He'd say / *for the love of God*

[Jesus is my best girl friend, my dutch boy]

I ask him *why me?* Beg, *can't I be normal in one way?* It weighs
him down, our hate, makes his shoulders sag, his back bend.
He touches the slits on my arms where I try to bleed out
the worst of me, slumps, bone-tired, looks me in the eye
and says, *Love, don't break the yolk.*

And the Word Was God

In the beginning was the word and the word was FAT
in the beginning I was fat   in the beginning I was lean &
long carried two weeks past due & wore preemie clothes & then I
chunked up   baby fat   a fat baby   baby I grew big
grew big boned   grew six inches taller than the other
little girls   grew hips & thighs & breasts before my time
in percentile on all the doctors' charts   I grew   I knew
I was too large   too loud too mouthy for boys
I knew even then I loved girls   I knew I knew I knew
by how loud the boys said no   I wanted them to say no
      I wanted them to say
yes   I wanted to feel like I could stop
burying myself in my body   my body grew large
my body grew larger   a walk-in closet   I stood on the inside
hiding behind dresses   on the outside   Bible verses
& Jesus   men who made sure I heard them tell me
my body was not my own   my mind was not my own
but it was it was it was   so I started to drag myself out
I kicked that door   open   I kicked it down
haven't looked back look   don't look back   don't look
back at the beginning   in the beginning was that word
      and that word was God   the word is not God
I am God   I am that word   I am God's
word   I am still   fat

WWJD / at the bar

Jesus would take one look at her / suck in air / breathe out *daaammnn* /
she's cute / *why you standing here* / *sis* / *go talk to her* / *ask for her number* /
Jesus would scribble his own / crooked on a cocktail napkin / Jesus would
slide it her way / give her a slow wink / *I want to get to know you* / *honey* /
let me buy you a drank

[Jesus and I are on a break]

Meanwhile, a blonde walked in wearing royal
blue leggings & I'm in love with her.
Her thighs—the way they slope out on the sides,
fat tugging muscle—there's a healthy curve there
in the back that stretches up to an ass that will fill
my hand, help me pull her close. Her leggings remind me
of a woman I met at a workshop, the way
her eyes explode when she's excited, the way her body flexes
when she moves, and the last time I saw her, the weight
she gained looked good, real good, and I should
text her, but there's a bank teller who wears ties
every day and always says hi, even if she's working the window
while I'm at the counter and I want to tell her I'd jump
that tall counter if she'd say yes to coffee with me,
but right now my coffee has gone cold. A youth pastor
at the table next to me says, "You should be thinking about boys"
to a young woman. I'm not. She's getting ministered to
and looks awful cute in her Buddy Holly glasses
& Chuck Taylors; I'd like to do this thing on purpose:
scoot my chair right over there, let my hands show her
all the things she could think about and feel,
things a hell of a lot more fun than boys. Meanwhile Jesus,
camped out across the table from me, looks up from his novel
& latte, says *Girl, you won't know until you try.*

Jesus and I Went to the Walmart

It was late, and what I really needed was some Epsom salts to soak
my ache. I've been dog-tired since I started exercising every day,
and you know I took on that part-time job cause you can't really
make good money at teaching & living in the city is rough. It
costs a lot to keep up.

Anyway, we snuck in on the pharmacy side, past the display of
cold & flu medicine and cough drops. I got my salts and figured
I may as well go ahead & pick up some lady plugs since I was
already here & had a coupon for Tampax Pearl.

I was trying to decide between the active super or the super
plus cause I could tell by the way I was craving a hamburger it
was going to be a bloody time of the month. Jesus gets a little
embarrassed by the lady juice, so he wandered off & next thing I
knew there he was in the condom aisle.

He'd cornered some young gun who kept walking past the
rubbers, trying to side-eye the different brands. He'd just about
settled on the ultra-thin when Jesus found him, took him by the
shoulder and started talking about how to please his girl. Jesus
held the ultra-ribbed and had just said something about clitoral
stimulation & remembering this wasn't a 50-yard dash when I
said, *Jesus, what* are *you doing?* and snapped the condoms out of his
hand.

Honey, [Jesus gets all solemn when he calls me honey,] *you know
he's gonna do it anyway, so he may as well be smart about it.*

Jesus took the condoms, handed them to the boy, said, *don't you
knock that girl up.*

Poor feller didn't know what'd hit him. He couldn't get to the
checkout line fast enough.

Jesus bought me a burger on the way home, and as we sat outside at the picnic tables, I said, *people around here are either afraid of having sex or afraid of people finding out they're having sex. Why do you reckon that is? Is it cause of religion?*

He took a long swallow and said, *no. It's desire, I think. The only feeling stronger than desire is fear, and most often we're afraid of the things we want so badly.*

Jesus, do you really think that's true?

Of course. Why do you think it took you so long to come out?

Damn. I hate it when he's right.

WWJD / about letting go

Jesus would say / *love* / *ask her to not forget* / *hook her*
from behind / *mouth hasped at her neck* / *her thighs*
will miss this / *nuzzle face* / *between lips* /
love / *teach her to drape* / *her dreams on you* /
eager / *like legs over shoulders*

Jesus Signs Me Up For a Dating App

Listen, he says, *there's no use wasting time
on that Tinder bullshit. You ain't interested
in any dick pics, so you may as well pick
the app for lezzies. Find at least one full body
photo. No point in hiding now. Use that one—
the one where you're wearing the necktie
and smiling real big—honey, if that don't
woo 'em, nothing will.*

WWJD / about my fat body

Her wet desire surprises me   the first time   I touch her
I don't know   what I'm doing   my body does   Her
body   leans into mine   into my hand   between her
legs   I tilt my face   into hers   love to watch her
when I touch her   see   where she gasps or groans
I want her   want to do this   right   want her
to feel my love   my body   but I hold back
with my body   hide my thighs in bed   wear shorts
over sexy underwear   I want to hide   in the dark   look
at her in the light   I want   to be touched
I don't want   to be touched   I want her
to touch me   sometimes she touches me   & I repeat
to myself   *it's her it's her it's her*   it's me
my mind perches on the line   between woods & yard
I know the threat   is not here   she is not
the raised fist   or tongue-lashing   or the you-have-to-
take-it! She loves me   my fat body   loves to touch me
I want to touch her   more   touch her   with more of me
it's her it's her it's her   I panic   afraid   this is all I'll ever offer.

WhatifIamnotenough?

                         I ask Jesus   when we grab coffee
He says   *(every kiss   is a step every touch*
a promise)   says one thing   and then   *the next*
I say   I'm afraid   I say   afraid   to let her
love on all of me yet.   My shame has not uncoiled.
Nonsense   he says   *let that shit go   Let her*
feel you.   This woman   She loves you   You've got one
life   One life to fill   with all the love   it can hold   Don't
spill it   *Come on   Don't fuck it up now.*

63

Jesus shouts, *Amen!*

I like the way boxer briefs feel—sleek, easy—under skinny jeans. Smooth,
my love trails her fingers along the elastic edges, along the softest parts
of me. She's never asked why I sometimes prefer this underwear,
and when I shaved part of my head, she said I was *hot*. My love
runs her tongue along my chest, up my back, the softest
parts of me. She touches my body and my body, the softest,
craves her touch. Her thighs grip my thighs, her face burrows
in my breasts. She holds me, locks her arms and legs around me,
holds me close, even when I cry. My body is a holler I've tried to escape
time and again, but now, with this woman, I am home.

WWJD / about love

You see her ass in front of you, reach out,
cup her curves in your palm. Latch yourself
there: her hip a hinge, her lips a door
you want to open and visit, not visit,
set up shop. You want to live there. You don't
have to imagine you're male. You don't need
a dick to be loved. Hold on. Her hip a hinge.
Her lips a door. Swing yourself into her
love. Breathe deep [through your mouth]—
let her thighs hold you close.

[Jesus rides shotgun]

We go balls to the wall,
                      windows down,
aviator sunglasses always on.
                            I drive like a bat
out of hell, do donuts
                   on sun-dry highways,

180s on ice-slick parkways. Sometimes
                          when I drift, I think
this is the end.

I used to be afraid. Sometimes
                         I still am. Maybe.

Don't hit the brakes, Jesus says.
                   Turn the wheel. That's how you know
                   the way you want to go.

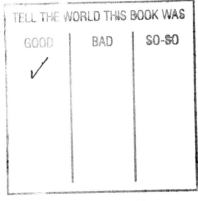

ACKNOWLEDGMENTS

The following poems have been published, in some form or another, by the kind and gracious editors of the following literary magazines/journals:

Appalachian Heritage—"*What We Tell Ourselves*" and "*[Jesus Rides Shotgun]*"

If You Can Hear This: Poems in Protest of an American Inauguration (Sibling Rivalry Press)—"*When Those Who Have the Power Start to Lose it, They Panic*"

Still: The Journal—"*Cant*" and "*Thirst*"

LGBTQ Fiction and Poetry from Appalachia (West Virginia University Press)—"*WWJD / about love,*" "*WWJD / about letting go,*" "*Jesus and I went to the Walmart,*" "*Catfisting,*" "*Pork Belly,*" "*A List of Times I Thought I Was Gay,*" and "*Jesus Signs Me Up for a Dating App*"

Talking River— "*I Wanted You to Fuck Me,*" "*Rain, Love,*" and "*Wannabe*"

The Louisville Review—"*Finished*" and "*WWJD/ on prayer*"

The Offing—"*All I Know of Coal*"

Waxwing—"*Baby, You're a Blight,*" "*Darling, You're a Stain,*" and "*Love Letter to the Boys in the First Class I Ever Taught*"

Notes:
"What We Tell Ourselves" quotes Job 28:9-12.
"After Seeing a Topo Map of my Childhood Stomping Grounds Hanging in a Colleague's Home" is for Jenny Williams.

GRATITUDE

I must thank the people who have read my work and championed me every step of the way.

Rebecca Gayle Howell, you taught me to write and live as my true self, and I am grateful to you for helping me unleash my voice and for showing me I have a right to exist. I will always have jars of home-canned tomatoes with your name on them.

Thank you to Kathleen Driskell for your guidance and keen eye as I pushed this book into fruition. I love you.

Thank you to my writing group and partners in crime, Jay McCoy, Keith Stewart, and Avery M. Guess, who have read my work, pushed me, and seen me through so many periods of growth in my person and my writing.

There is a group of writers, editors, and friends who have supported my work, talked me through revisions, and offered love and encouragement, and I need to thank them all: Silas House, Jason Howard, George Ella Lyon, Maurice Manning, Carter Sickels, Marianne Worthington, Justin Bigos, Bryan Borland, Rebecca Hazelwood, Seth Pennington, Amanda Jo Runyon, Julie Marie Wade, Denton Loving, and Shawna Kay Rodenberg.

Thank you to my Appalachian Writers' Workshop family at the Hindman Settlement School. Everyone I've worked with in and out of workshop there has informed my writing.

This book wouldn't have been possible without the financial support of the Money for Women/Barbara Deming Memorial Fund, Inc. and The Kentucky Foundation for Women.

Thank you to the late Mary Ellen Miller, a fierce woman and teacher—a spitfire who always asked, What are you writing? The writing was the point, always. You were the first to guide me and your voice stays with me.

And finally, thank you to Ashley, who has supported me, cheered me on, and, most importantly, loved me in a deep and lasting way. It's grace that we found each other, and my home is by your side.

One more! Thank you, reader, for choosing my book. Whoever you are, I hope something in these pages helps you find a way to live your truth.

ABOUT THE POET

Savannah Sipple is a writer from east Kentucky. Her poems have recently been published in *Appalachian Heritage*, *Waxwing*, *Talking River*, *The Offing*, and *The Louisville Review*. She is also the recipient of grants from the Money for Women/ Barbara Deming Memorial Fund and the Kentucky Foundation for Women. She currently resides in Lexington, Kentucky, with her partner, Ashley.

www.savannahsipple.com

ABOUT THE PRESS

Sibling Rivalry Press is an independent press based in Little Rock, Arkansas. It is a sponsored project of Fractured Atlas, a nonprofit arts service organization. Contributions to support the operations of Sibling Rivalry Press are tax-deductible to the extent permitted by law, and your donations will directly assist in the publication of work that disturbs and enraptures. To contribute to the publication of more books like this one, please visit our website and click donate.

Sibling Rivalry Press gratefully acknowledges the following donors, without whom this book would not be possible:

Tony Taylor
Mollie Lacy
Karline Tierney
Maureen Seaton
Travis Lau
Michael Broder & Indolent Books
Robert Petersen
Jennifer Armour
Alana Smoot
Paul Romero
Julie R. Enszer
Clayton Blackstock
Tess Wilmans-Higgins & Jeff Higgins
Sarah Browning
Tina Bradley
Kai Coggin
Queer Arts Arkansas
Jim Cory
Craig Cotter
Hugh Tipping
Mark Ward

Russell Bunge
Joe Pan & Brooklyn Arts Press
Carl Lavigne
Karen Hayes
J. Andrew Goodman
Diane Greene
W. Stephen Breedlove
Ed Madden
Rob Jacques
Erik Schuckers
Sugar le Fae
John Bateman
Elizabeth Ahl
Risa Denenberg
Ron Mohring & Seven Kitchens Press
Guy Choate & Argenta Reading Series
Guy Traiber
Don Cellini
John Bateman
Gustavo Hernandez
Anonymous (12)